Saint Thérèse of Lisieux

Saint Thérèse of Lisieux
of Lisieux

In My Own Words

Compiled by Judith A. Bauer

Liguori

LIGUORI, MISSOURI

Imprimi Potest: Thomas D. Picton, C.Ss.R.
Provincial, Denver Province, The Redemptorists

Published by Liguori Publications, Liguori, Missouri
www.liguori.org

Library of Congress Cataloging-in-Publication Data

Thérèse of Lisieux, Saint, 1873–1897.
    [Selections. English. 2005]
    Thérèse of Lisieux : in my own words / compiled by Judith
A. Bauer.—1st ed.
       p. cm.
    ISBN 0-7648-1340-4
    1. Spiritual life—Catholic Church. I. Bauer, Judy, 1941–
II. Title.

BX4700.T5A25 2005
282'.092—dc22
[B]   2005044361

Quotations in this book are from *Saint Thérèse of Lisieux, The
Little Flower of Jesus*, translated by Thomas N. Taylor. New York:
P. J. Kenedy & Sons, 1926.

Photographs courtesy of Office Central Lisieux, 51, rue du
Carmel, 14100 Lisieux, France. Used with permission.

Printed in the United States of America
09 08 07 06 05   5 4 3 2 1
First edition

CONTENTS

Introduction vii

Chronology of Sainthood xvii

Embraced by God's Mercy 1

Immersed in the Words of the Gospel 9

Awed by God's Image in Nature 13

Practiced in Poverty, Chastity, and Obedience 19

Schooled in Prayer 27

Transformed in the Crucible of Suffering 35

Abandoned to the Will of God 51

Devoted to Love of God 61

Humbly Hidden in the Heart of God 77

Secluded in the Little Way 89

Dedicated to Our Lady 107

Accomplished in the Small Ways
of Self-Denial 115

$\mathcal{I}$NTRODUCTION

Marie Françoise Thérèse Martin was born on January 2, 1873, in Alençon, a small town in the Normandy region of France. She was the last of nine children born to Louis Martin, a skilled jeweler and watchmaker, and Zélie Guérin Martin, an accomplished lacemaker. Thérèse was baptized on January 4, 1873, with her then-thirteen-year-old sister, Marie, as godmother. Shortly after her birth she contracted an illness that prevented her from eating, and she was sent away to the small hamlet of Sémallé to receive special nursing care. There she stayed, separated from her mother, for the course of a year, until April 1874. In celebration of her return home in April 1874, Thérèse's mother made her a beautiful sky-blue dress with a white coat, the colors of the Blessed Virgin.

The saint's early childhood was spent in the warm intimacy of a deeply pious family, where prayer, the liturgy, and good works formed the fabric of a Christian household. Their faith and good works, known then as "practices," were carried out each day in conjunction with praying the rosary, affectionately called "pearls." According to them, the "practices" and "pearls" were faith offerings intended to adorn the crown that would be given to the Lord after death.

At the tender age of four, Thérèse had to battle another illness, only this time it was her mother who suffered with an advanced and untreatable form of breast cancer. Her mother's cancer advanced rapidly, and she died in August 1877, leaving her husband to raise their five surviving daughters (four of Thérèse's siblings had died young). Before her death, Thérèse's mother predicted her daughter's path in her last correspondence: "My Thérèse is a charming little creature; I assure you that this one will manage well." But not without some grave obstacles along the way!

Shortly after the death of her mother, the family moved to a fine house in Lisieux named *Les Buissonnets* (The Hedges) where Thérèse's sisters, Marie and Pauline, functioned as her secondary mothers and attended to her education. Still shocked by the death of her mother, Thérèse turned into a shy and introverted child. She described herself in her autobiography as "timid and retiring, sensitive to an excessive degree."

Thérèse spent the five years from 1881 to 1886 attending the Benedictine Abbey school of Notre-Dame du Pré. She declared these five years as the "saddest of my life." She worked hard to become an outstanding student, loved catechism, history, and science, but made no friends outside of her family circle. In fact, her competence incited envy and teasing among her schoolmates.

At the age of ten, Thérèse fell into a deep depression when her sister Pauline left the household to become a Carmelite (Sister Agnes of Jesus). The shock of losing her second mother went so deep that Thérèse fell seriously ill, suffering hallucinations, severe headaches, and insomnia. No one could find an explanation for Thérèse's illness. When it seemed that she was close to death, the family's statue of the Blessed Virgin, which was in her room, appeared to smile at her, and she was miraculously cured.

Once Thérèse regained her health, she started preparations for her long-anticipated first Communion. She received the Eucharist for the first time on May 8, 1884, followed the next month by the sacrament of confirmation. This period provided a spiritual respite for Thérèse, until a retreat initiated a severe case of scruples that lasted more than a year. The scruples were so debilitating that Thérèse was removed from school. She lived in constant fear of sinning and cried so much that some thought she "would have no tears to shed later on!"

In the midst of Thérèse's spiritual torment, her sister Marie, taking the name Sister Marie of the Sacred Heart, also entered the Lisieux Carmel. This was too much for the thirteen-year-old Thérèse, who had now lost a third mother. Marie had been her confidant and had helped her handle her scrupulosity. By now Thérèse was a tall, attractive young woman, with blue eyes and beautiful blond hair. Even so, her inner anguish was only abated when she appealed to her sister and four brothers in heaven to intercede for her.

After midnight Mass on Christmas 1886, Thérèse's hypersensitivity, depression, outbursts of tears, and self-doubt were suddenly lifted from her, leaving her in possession of a new inner peace. The strong character that she had possessed at the age of four, prior to the death of her mother, returned to her. Now the little saint could forget herself and work to fulfill her dream of entering the Carmelite Order as soon as possible.

During the year of 1887, Thérèse fought with great determination to achieve her goal of entering the Order at the age of fifteen. This was a year of enormous spiritual development as she fought to win the approval of her father (easily persuaded) and to overcome the objections of her uncle Isadore Guérin (initially opposed but won over by psychological pressure from Pauline), the canon of the Lisieux Carmel (adamantly opposed), and the Bishop of Bayeux (who took Thérèse's request under advisement).

Shortly after her appeal to the Bishop of Bayeux, Thérèse, her father, and her sister Céline embarked on a pilgrimage to Rome where Thérèse was determined to approach Pope Leo XIII himself. After traveling throughout France, Switzerland, and much of Italy, the Martin entourage arrived in Rome. Thérèse's meeting with Leo XIII occurred on Sunday, November 20, 1887. Though it was formally forbidden for anyone to speak to the Pope, Thérèse was granted the opportunity, and she asked Leo XIII for a "great favor." She requested his permission to enter the Carmel of Lisieux. Taken by surprise, the Holy Father murmured that he did not understand. He turned to the priest, Father Révérony, who was in charge of the group, who explained: "Most Holy Father, it is a child who wishes to enter Carmel at the age of fifteen; however, the superiors are examining the question at this moment." Reassured, the Pope turned to Thérèse and said, "My child, do as the superiors tell you to. You will enter Carmel if the Good Lord wishes it."

After a tense and difficult wait, Thérèse received permission from the Bishop of Bayeux (thus overruling the canon of the Carmel) to enter the Lisieux Carmel. Still, she had to wait until Easter because the prioress wanted to spare her the rigors of Lent. Finally, on April 9, 1888, at the age of fifteen, Thérèse Martin entered the Carmel enclosure to join twenty-four other companions.

Sister Thérèse of the Child Jesus (she later added "of the Holy Face" to her religious name) was delighted with her lot, even though she encountered more thorns than roses: intense cold, a rigid and Spartan diet, difficulties of prayer, lack of sleep, and clashes of community life. Nevertheless, after a retreat marked by intense spiritual aridity, Thérèse took the habit of a Carmelite novice on January 10, 1889.

Early in religious life she was challenged by a heretical religious movement known as

Jansenism that affected the community by overemphasizing predestination, human depravity, and moral rigorism—a theology that seemed to feed upon her overscrupulous past. However, she found relief through the writings of John of the Cross' *Spiritual Canticle* and *Living Flame of Love*. Here was the "Living Saint of Love," the trailblazer of the path she was meant to follow. A great peace came over her when she at last made her profession on September 8, 1890—taking the black veil in a public ceremony, and asking of Jesus "may creatures be nothing for me and may I be nothing for them, but you, Jesus, be everything."

After making her final profession, Thérèse's spiritual progress continued, and her sense of her own "littleness" grew deeper. She said: "It is impossible for me to grow up, so I must bear with myself such as I am with all my imperfections. But I want to seek out a means of going to heaven by a little way, a way that is very straight, very short, and totally new." Convinced that God would enable her to become a saint and to "climb the steep ladder of holiness," her spirit rose up on the wings of her "Divine Eagle." Having discovered the treasures of God's "Merciful Love," she gave herself to him at the Mass of the Trinity on June 9, 1895.

Thérèse had numerous responsibilities at the Carmel of Lisieux. The prioress, Mother Agnes of Jesus—who was actually Thérèse's biological sister Pauline—asked her to write verses and theatrical entertainments for liturgical celebrations. Thérèse happily wrote two plays about Saint Joan of Arc—even performing in them with great effect. Mother Agnes also required Thérèse to write down her "childhood memories." Thérèse obeyed, creating an eighty-six-page notebook ("Manuscript A"), in which she saw herself as a "little white flower" that had grown under the rays of the Divine Sun. Soon after finishing her first writing, Thérèse was entrusted with the care of the other novices and instructed to become a spiritual correspondent to two missionary priests who were destined for service in China and Africa.

By Good Friday of 1896, Thérèse showed the first signs of tuberculosis and suffered two episodes of coughing up blood. She saw these hemorrhages as a summons from the Lord to join him in heaven. After Easter, she was overcome by a "dark night of the soul," a "fog," which was to last, with only brief periods of reprieve, until she died. Thérèse turned this trial of faith into a time of atonement, agreeing to remain in this darkness so that others more needy would receive the Light.

Shortly thereafter, Thérèse was overcome by powerful desires to become a priest, prophet, Doctor of the Church, missionary, and a martyr. Inspired by a passage in the writings of Saint Paul, she discovered that her true vocation was to be Love in the heart of the Church, and that by living this vocation she could "be everything." Writing down these thoughts for her sister and her godmother—known as Sister Marie of the Sacred Heart—she produced what is now called "Manuscript B." The wish to save souls never left her, and she seriously considered an evangelical mission to the Carmelites in Vietnam, but she was prevented from doing this on account of her deteriorating health.

The tuberculosis gained ground silently. Early in 1897, Thérèse felt that she had not long to live. By April she was forced to remain either in her cell or in the garden, and, by June, the prioress Mother Marie de Gonazga ordered Thérèse to finish writing down her thoughts and observations. She wrote an additional thirty-six pages in a little black notebook. This manuscript, known as "Manuscript C," became the third and final part of her autobiography.

Ordered to the infirmary on July 8, Thérèse coughed blood, slept little, and was unable to eat. Medications were of little help. With great pain, she wrote her last letters to her spiritual brothers and sisters. She was worn out, but never lost her serenity or good humor. At the tender age of twenty-four, she died on Thursday, September 30, 1897, whispering "My God, I love You!"

CHRONOLOGY
OF SAINTHOOD

1898: First publication of Thérèse's autobiography; 2,000 copies printed.

1899: First visitors come to Thérèse's grave, seeking her intercession.

1908: Young blind girl from Lisieux is cured at her grave.

1910: Bishop of Bayeux begins process of canonization.

1915: Process of sainthood for Thérèse is submitted to Rome.

1921: Benedict XV declares Thérèse a Venerable Servant of God.

1923: Pius XI beatifies Sister Thérèse of the Child Jesus.

1925: Only twenty-eight years after her death, when she would have been fifty-two years old, Thérèse declared a saint.

1927: Thérèse, along with Saint Francis Xavier, declared patroness of the missions.

1997: Thérèse declared a doctor of the Church, proclaimed Doctor of Confidence and Missionaries.

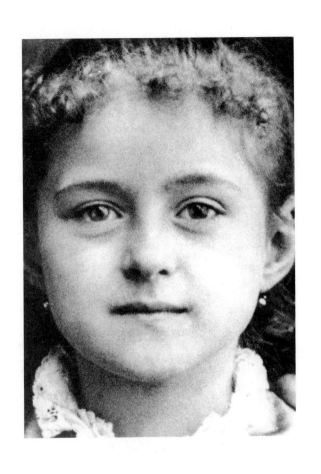

EMBRACED BY
GOD'S MERCY

Embraced by God's Mercy

At the beginning of her autobiography, Thérèse struggles to set out the theme of her life and puts down her thoughts on the graces that God has granted her. The writing of the story of her soul, initiated and completed under obedience to her superior, is done in the light of her strong and enduring belief in God's divine mercy.

I begin the story of my soul by singing what must be my eternal song: "The mercies of the Lord."

MANUSCRIPT A

Opening the Gospels, my eyes fell on these words: "He went up to the mountain and called to him those whom he wanted" (Mark 3:13). They threw a clear light on the mystery of my vocation and of my entire life, but above all upon the favors Our Lord has granted to my soul. He does not call those who are worthy, but those whom he will. Saint Paul says, quoting God's words to Moses, "I will have mercy on whom I will have mercy" (Romans 9:15).

MANUSCRIPT A

To me [Our Lord] has indeed been always "compassionate and merciful, long-suffering and plenteous in mercy" (Psalms 103:8). So it gives me great joy, dear Mother, [Thérèse's sister Pauline, Mother Agnes of Jesus and prioress of the Carmel of Lisieux at the time of her writing] to come to you and sing of his unspeakable mercies.

MANUSCRIPT A

The flower [Thérèse titled the first part of her autobiography "The Story of the Springtime of a Little White Flower"] now telling her tale rejoices in having to publish the wholly undeserved favors of Our Lord. She knows that in herself she had nothing worthy of attracting him; his mercy it was that filled her with good things—his mercy alone....In his love he willed to preserve her from the poisoned breath of the world, for hardly had her petals unfolded when this good Master transplanted her to the mountain of Carmel.

MANUSCRIPT A

It is so easy to go astray along the world's seductive paths. Without doubt the sweetness which it offers to one somewhat advanced in virtue is always mingled with bitterness, nor can the immense void of such a soul's desires be filled by the flattery of a moment; had the world smiled on me from the cradle, there is no knowing what I might have become. How gratefully, then, dearest Mother, do I sing "the mercies of the Lord."

MANUSCRIPT A

On this most radiant night [Christmas 1886] began the third period of my life, the most beautiful of all. Satisfied with my good will, Our Lord accomplished in an instant the work I had not been able to do during years. Like the Apostles, I might have said: "Master, we have labored all night and have taken nothing" (Luke 5:5). More merciful to me than to His beloved disciples, Jesus took the net, and casting it, drew it out full of fishes: He made me a fisher of men. Love and a spirit of self-forgetfulness took complete possession of my heart, and thenceforward I was perfectly happy.

MANUSCRIPT A

$\mathcal{D}$ear Mother [Thérèse's sister Pauline, Mother Agnes of Jesus], after so many graces may I not sing with the psalmist that "the Lord is good…"? It seems to me that if every soul were to receive such favors God would be loved to excess and feared by none; I believe that every least willful fault would be avoided out of love, without thought of fear.

Yet all souls cannot be alike. They must suffer, so that each divine perfection may receive special honor. To me he has manifested his infinite mercy and in this resplendent mirror I contemplate his other attributes. There, each appears radiant with *love*.

MANUSCRIPT A

$\mathcal{G}$od's Merciful Love renews and purifies me, cleansing my soul from all trace of sin. I do not fear Purgatory, for though I know I do not deserve even to enter with the Holy Souls into that place of expiation, I also know that the fire of Love is more sanctifying than the fire of Purgatory, that Jesus could not will useless suffering for us.

MANUSCRIPT A

*W*hile thinking one day of those who offer themselves as victims to the Justice of God, and who turn aside the punishment due to sinners, taking it upon themselves, I felt such an offering to be both noble and generous. I was very far, nevertheless, from feeling myself drawn to make it, and from the depths of my heart I cried: "O my Divine Master, shall your justice alone find atoning victims? Has not your Merciful Love need of them also? On every side it is ignored and rejected…those hearts on which you would lavish it turn to creatures and seek their happiness in the miserable satisfaction of a moment, rather than cast themselves into your arms—into the ecstatic fires of your infinite love."

MANUSCRIPT A

*I*t is not merely because I have been preserved from mortal sin that I lift up my heart to God in trust and in love. I am certain that even if I had on my conscience every imaginable crime, I should lose nothing of my confidence, but would throw myself, my heart broken with sorrow, into the arms of my Savior. I remember His love for the prodigal son, I have heard His words to Saint Mary

Magdalene, to the woman taken in adultery,
and the women of Samaria. No—there is no
one who could frighten me, for I know too well
what to believe concerning His Mercy and His
Love.

MANUSCRIPT B

O my God…you know how often I lose
sight of what is my only care, and straying from
your side, allow my wings to be dragged in the
muddy pools of this world. Then "I cry like a
young swallow" (Isaiah 38:14) and my cry tells
you all, and you remember, O Infinite Mercy,
that "You did not come to call the just but
sinners" (Matthew 9:13).

MANUSCRIPT C

IMMERSED IN
THE WORDS
OF THE GOSPEL

Immersed in the Words of the Gospel

For Thérèse of Lisieux, the Scriptures are her direct contact with the word of God. Though she was devoted to Thomas à Kempis' Imitation of Christ at the age of fourteen, she used it as a steppingstone to the Scriptures. She always carried a copy of the New Testament around with her. She often spent time in her cell writing out quotations from Scripture, in essence making her own index. Indeed, she quotes Our Lord's words to Saint Gertrude: "Search out for yourself those of my words which breathe the most love, write them down, treasure them as a sacred relic and read them often."

For a long time I sustained my spiritual life on the "fine flour" contained in the *Imitation of Christ*. It was the only book from which I derived any good, because as yet I had not discovered the treasures hidden in the Holy Gospels. I always carried it about with me, much to the amusement of those at home, and my aunt would often open it, making me repeat the first chapter upon which she chanced to light.

MANUSCRIPT A

10

In my helplessness, the Holy Scriptures and the *Imitation* are of the greatest assistance; I find in them a hidden manna, pure and genuine. It is from the Gospels, however, that I derive the most help in time of prayers; I find in their pages all that my poor soul needs, and I am always discovering there new lights and hidden mysterious meanings.

MANUSCRIPT A

I cannot always, indeed, carry out to the letter the words of the Gospel, for occasions arise when I am compelled to refuse a request. Yet, when charity has taken deep root in the soul, it shows itself outwardly, and there is always a way of refusing so graciously what one cannot give, that the refusal affords as much pleasure as the gift itself.

MANUSCRIPT B

Since Our Lord is in heaven I can only follow him by the traces of light and fragrance which he has left behind him. But as soon as I open the Holy Gospels, I breathe the perfume exhaled by the life of Jesus, and I know which way to run. It is not to the highest place but to the lowest that I hasten.

MANUSCRIPT B

*L*ike the prophets and doctors, I would be a light unto souls. I would travel the world over to preach your name, O My Beloved....I would spread the Gospel in all parts of the earth, even to the farthest isles.

MANUSCRIPT C

*O*n earth, even in matters of Holy Scripture, our vision is dim. It distresses me to see the differences in its translations, and had I been a priest I would have learned Hebrew, so as to read the Word of God as He deigned to utter it in human speech.

COUNSELS

Awed by God's Image in Nature

Awed by God's Image in Nature

Thérèse saw the world around her in the light of God's almighty power. She thought of God as watching over all that happens, and from whom nothing is hidden. Nature was a key that helped Thérèse unlock the truths of God's love.

*O*ur Lord…showed me the book of Nature, and I understood that every flower created by him is beautiful, that the brilliance of the rose and the whiteness of the lily do not lessen the perfume of the violet or the sweet simplicity of the daisy.

MANUSCRIPT A

*A*s the sun shines both on the cedar and on the smallest flower, so the Divine Sun illumines each soul, great or lowly, and all things work together for its good, just as in Nature the seasons are so arranged that on the appointed day the humblest daisy will unfold its petals.

MANUSCRIPT A

If a little flower could speak, it seems to me that it would tell quite simply what God had done for it, without hiding any of its gifts. It would not say, under the pretext of humility, that it was not pretty and did not have a sweet scent, that the sun had withered its petals or the storm bruised its stem—if it knew such were not the case.

MANUSCRIPT A

How sweet the memories [of early childhood]....Indeed, I can still feel the vivid impressions made on my childish heart by the vision of the cornfields studded with cornflowers, poppies, and marguerites. Even at that age I loved far-stretching views, sunlit spaces, and stately trees: in a word all the beauties of Nature cast their spell upon me and raised my soul to heaven.

MANUSCRIPT A

If Our Lord had not lavished his sunshine upon his Little Flower [Thérèse], she never could have become acclimated to this earth. Still too weak to bear either rain or storm, she needed warmth, refreshing dew, and gentle breezes—gifts never denied her, even in the wintry season of trials.

MANUSCRIPT A

$\mathcal{O}$ne day when we [Thérèse and her father] were out, angry clouds darkened the lovely blue sky, and a storm, accompanied by vivid lightning, rumbled overhead. I looked around on every side so as to miss nothing of the splendid scene. A thunderbolt fell in a field close by, and far from being the least bit frightened, I was overjoyed—God seemed so near.

MANUSCRIPT A

$\mathcal{I}$ was six or seven when I saw the sea for the first time. I could not turn my eyes away: its majesty, the roaring of the waves, the whole vast spectacle impressed me deeply and spoke to my soul of God's power and greatness.

MANUSCRIPT A

$\mathcal{A}$t the hour when the sun seems to sink into the broad expanse of waters, leaving behind it a trail of light, I sat with you [her sister Pauline] on a lonely rock and let my gaze linger on this path of splendor. You described it as an image of grace illumining the way of faithful hearts here on earth. Then I pictured my own soul as a tiny boat, with graceful white sails, floating in the midst of the golden stream, and I determined never to steer it out of the sight of Jesus.

MANUSCRIPT A

I know that God has no need of anyone to help him in his work of sanctification, but just as he allows a clever gardener to cultivate rare and delicate plants, providing him with the necessary skill to accomplish it, while reserving to himself the task of making them grow, so also does he wish to be helped in the divine cultivation of souls.

MANUSCRIPT A

N othing at all frightens me, neither wind nor rain; and should impenetrable clouds conceal from my eyes the Divine Sun of Love, should it seem to me that beyond this life there is darkness only, this would be the hour of perfect joy, the hour in which to urge my confidence to its uttermost bounds, for knowing that beyond the dark clouds my Sun is still shining.

MANUSCRIPT C

PRACTICED IN POVERTY, CHASTITY, AND OBEDIENCE

Practiced in Poverty, Chastity, and Obedience

When Thérèse entered the Carmel at Lisieux at the age of fifteen, she exchanged her earthly possessions for the vows of poverty, chastity, and obedience. Thérèse clearly believed that the practice of these monastic virtues was an important aid in living a life conformed to the will of God.

Poverty

Death has come to many I knew then—young, rich, and happy. I call to mind their luxurious homes, and ask myself where they are now, and what profit they now derive from the mansions and estates where I saw them enjoying all the good things of life. Then I reflect that "all is vanity" except loving God and serving him alone.

MANUSCRIPT A

Since the day of my clothing I had received abundant lights on religious perfection and particularly on the vow of poverty. While I was a postulant I liked to have nice things for my own use, and to find what was needed ready to hand. Jesus bore with me patiently. He does not disclose everything at once to souls, but as a rule gives his light little by little.

MANUSCRIPT A

One evening, after Compline, I searched in vain for my lamp on the shelves where they are kept. I concluded rightly that a Sister had taken it believing it to be her own, and during the time of the "Great Silence" I could not ask to have it back. Must I then remain in darkness for a whole hour, just when I had counted on doing a great deal of work? Without the interior light of grace I should undoubtedly have pitied myself, but in the midst of the darkness I found my soul divinely illumined. It was brought home to me that poverty consists in being deprived not only of what is convenient but also of what is necessary, so that I felt happy instead of aggrieved.

MANUSCRIPT A

*W*hen God tells me to give to anyone who asks of me, and to allow what is mine to be taken without asking for it back, it seems to me that He speaks not only of the things of earth but also of the goods of heaven. Neither the one nor the other are really mine; I renounced the first by the vow of poverty and the others are gifts which are simply lent.

MANUSCRIPT B

*J*esus does not wish me to reclaim what belongs to me. This ought to appear quite natural, since in reality I own nothing, and ought to rejoice when an occasion brings home to me the poverty to which I am solemnly vowed. Formerly, I used to think myself detached from everything, but since Our Lord's words have become clear, I see how imperfect I am.

MANUSCRIPT C

I am like the poor who hold out their hands for the necessaries of life and who if refused are not surprised, because no one owes them anything. To soar above all natural sentiment brings the deepest peace, nor is there any joy equal to that which is felt by the truly poor in spirit.

MANUSCRIPT C

Chastity

*O*bserving that some of the girls [at boarding school at the time of Thérèse's first Communion] were very devoted to one or another of the teachers, I tried to imitate them, but never succeeded in winning special favor. Happy failure, from how many evils have you not saved me! I am most thankful to Our Lord that he has allowed me to find only bitterness in earthly friendships. With a heart such as mine, I so easily could have been taken captive and had my wings clipped.

MANUSCRIPT A

I know well that Jesus saw I was too weak to be exposed to temptation, for without a doubt had my eyes been dazzled by the deceitful light of creatures, I should have been utterly lost.... Too well do I realize that without him I might have fallen as low as Saint Mary Magdalen.

MANUSCRIPT A

*O*n the morning of November 4, while Lisieux lay shrouded in the darkness of night, we passed through her silent streets [to begin a pilgrimage to Rome]....I was well aware that throughout the pilgrimage I should come across things that might disturb me, and having no knowledge of evil, I feared to discover it. As yet I had not experienced that "to the pure all things are pure" (Tobit 1:15)—that a simple soul does not see evil in anything, since evil exists only in impure hearts and not in inanimate objects.

MANUSCRIPT A

*T*hrough Chastity, I become the Sister of conquering Angels....Chastity conquers hearts at the request of my beloved King.

POEM 48

Obedience

*I*t is to you, dearest Mother [Thérèse's sister Pauline, Mother Agnes of Jesus] that I am about to confide the story of my soul. When you asked me to write it, I feared that the task might unsettle me, but Our Lord has made me understand that by simple obedience I will please him best.

MANUSCRIPT A

From how much disquiet and uneasiness do we free ourselves by the vow of obedience! Happy is the simple religious: her one guide being the will of her superiors, she is ever sure of following the right path, and has no fear of being misled, even when it may appear her superiors are mistaken.

MANUSCRIPT B

SCHOOLED
IN PRAYER

Schooled in Prayer

Thérèse's family organized themselves around the rhythms of the liturgical year, prayer, good works on behalf of the poor and the ill, and the strict observance of Church rules and regulations. Prayer took on a new aspect upon Thérèse's entry into Carmel. There she followed the strict rule laid down by Saint Teresa of Ávila—a rule, which included two hours of prayerful reflection each day, as well as the praying the Divine Office, Mass, an annual retreat, spiritual reading, and the saying of the commonly loved prayers of the time. Even with all these organized approaches, Thérèse found her own path to prayer.

Those were supremely happy days when my dear "King" [Thérèse's father] went fishing and took me with him. Sometimes I tried my hand with a small rod of my own, but more often I preferred to sit on the grass at some little distance. My reflections would then become really deep, and without knowing what meditation meant, my soul was absorbed in prayer. Far-off sounds wafted towards me;…the earth seemed a land of exile, and I dreamed of Heaven.

MANUSCRIPT A

*A*t that time [when Thérèse was preparing for her first Communion], I would have liked to practice mental prayer, but Marie [her sister] thought it better that I should keep to vocal prayer only….While I was at school at the Abbey, one of the teachers asked me what I did on holidays when I stayed at home. I answered timidly: "I often hide in a corner of my room, where I can shut myself in with the bed-curtains, and then I think." "But what do you think about?" she said. "I think about God, about the shortness of life, about eternity…." It is clear to me now that I was then really engaged in mental prayer under God's gentle guidance.

Manuscript A

*H*ere [in the chapel before the Blessed Sacrament], I found my one consolation. Was not Jesus my only friend? To Him alone I could open my heart. All conversations with creatures, even on holy subjects, wearied me.

Manuscript A

I was consumed with an insatiable thirst for souls, and I longed at any cost to snatch them from the everlasting flames of hell. About this time, a notorious criminal, Pranzini, had been condemned to death for several horrible murders. He was impenitent, and in consequence it was feared he would be eternally lost. Longing to avert that greatest of misfortunes, I employed all the spiritual means I could think of to obtain the ransom of this poor sinner; and knowing that of myself I could do nothing, I offered up the infinite merits of Our Savior together with the treasures of Holy Church.

In the depths of my heart, I said with all simplicity: "My God, I am sure You will pardon this unhappy Pranzini, and I shall still think so even if he does not confess his sins or give any sign of sorrow."

…My prayer was granted to the letter…. Without confession or absolution Pranzini had mounted the scaffold, and the executioners were dragging him towards the fatal block, when, all at once, apparently in answer to a sudden inspiration, he turned around, seized a crucifix which the priest held toward him, and kissed Our Lord's Sacred Wounds three times!

Manuscript A

The power of prayer has been understood by all the saints, and especially, perhaps, by those who have illumined the world with the light of Christ's teaching....The Almighty has given them as a fulcrum to lean upon, Himself—*Himself alone*—and for a lever, the prayer that inflames with the fire of love.

MANUSCRIPT B

The power of prayer is indeed wonderful. It is like a queen, who having free access always to the king can obtain whatsoever she asks. To secure a hearing there is no need to recite set prayers composed for the occasion—were this the case I should indeed deserve to be pitied.

MANUSCRIPT B

Apart from the Divine Office, which in spite of my unworthiness is a daily joy, I have not the courage to search through books for beautiful prayers; they are so numerous that it would only make my head ache, and, besides, each one is more lovely than the other. Unable either to say them all or to choose between them, I do as a child would who cannot read—I say just what I want to say to God, quite simply, and He never fails to understand me.

MANUSCRIPT B

For me, prayer is an uplifting of the heart, a glance towards heaven, a cry of gratitude and of love in times of sorrow as well as of joy. It is something noble, something supernatural, which expands the soul and unites it to God.

MANUSCRIPT B

When my state of spiritual aridity is such that not a single good thought will come, I repeat very slowly the "Our Father" and the "Hail Mary," which are enough to console me, and to provide divine food for my soul.

MANUSCRIPT B

Since I have two brother missionaries, as well as my little Sisters the novices, the days would be too short to ask in detail for the needs of each soul, and I am afraid I might forget something important. Complicated methods are not for simple souls, and as I am one of these, Our Lord himself has inspired me with a very simple way of fulfilling my obligations.

One day, after Holy Communion, He made me understand these words of Solomon: "Draw me: we will run after You to the odor of Your ointments" (Song of Songs 1:4). My Jesus,

there is no need then to say: In drawing me,
draw also the souls that I love. The words
"draw me" are sufficient;...for all those whom I
love are drawn with me.

Manuscript B

*I*t is God's will that, here below, souls shall
distribute to one another by prayer the
heavenly treasures with which He has enriched
them. And this in order that, when they reach
their everlasting home, they may love one
another with grateful hearts and with an
affection far beyond that which reigns in the
most perfect family circle on earth.

Counsels

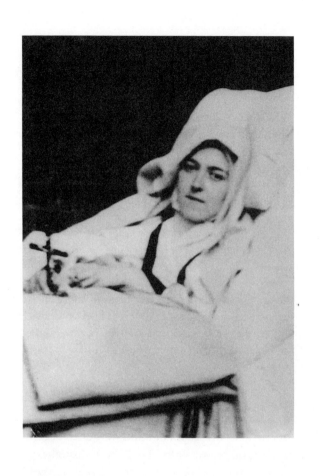

Transformed in
the Crucible
of Suffering

Transformed in the Crucible of Suffering

"Suffering" is not a word many people would apply to Thérèse of Lisieux. However, the young saint suffered a great deal and from a very early age. Her first trials came about at the age of four with the death of her mother, and her sufferings of both mental and physical sorts culminated with her heroic death from tuberculosis. In truth, Thérèse found treasures in suffering. She not only accepted her sufferings but came to long for them. On her deathbed, she said to her sister Mother Agnes of Jesus; "Since my first Communion, when I begged Jesus to change for me all earthly consolations into bitterness, I have always had a desire to suffer." These words would also seem to be directed at us who should see her sufferings as a beacon to turn our own sorrows into instruments of salvation.

*L*ater on, when the way of perfection was opened out before me, I realized that to become a saint, one must suffer much, one must always choose the most perfect path. I also understand that there are many degrees of holiness, each soul being free to respond to the calls of Our Lord, and to do much or little for His love—in a word, to select among the sacrifices He asks.

MANUSCRIPT A

*I*n the days of my childhood, I cried out: "My God, I choose everything—I will not be a saint by halves, I am not afraid of suffering for you."

MANUSCRIPT A

*W*ith Mama's death, I began the second period of my life, the most sorrowful of all....My naturally happy disposition deserted me. I became timid and shy, and so sensitive that a look was often sufficient to make me burst into tears.

MANUSCRIPT A

I told you once I should like to go away with you [Thérèse's sister Pauline, Mother Agnes of Jesus] to a far-off desert, and you replied that you wished it too, and would wait till I should be old enough to set out. I took this impossible promise in earnest, and great was my grief when I overheard you speaking to Marie about your approaching entrance into Carmel....How can I describe the anguish my heart endured! In a flash I beheld life as it really is, full of suffering and constant partings, and I shed most bitter tears.

MANUSCRIPT A

*I*t was during the retreat before my second Communion that I fell prey to scruples, and I remained in this unhappy state for nearly two years. It is not possible for me to describe all the sufferings it entailed; one must have passed through such a martyrdom to be able to understand it. [Thérèse became so ill that she was taken from school at the age of thirteen.]

MANUSCRIPT A

*B*efore sending a ray of hope to shine on my soul, God allowed me to pass through a three days' martyrdom....Never before had I so well understood the bitter sorrow of Our Lady and Saint Joseph as they walked through the streets of Jerusalem in search of the Divine Child. It was as if I were lost in some fearful desert; or rather my soul seemed like a frail skiff, without a pilot, left to the mercy of the stormy waters. [These trials occurred at the point when Thérèse's uncle refused his permission for her to enter Carmel.]

MANUSCRIPT A

*L*ater on, when the time of trial comes— when I am enclosed in Carmel and shall be able to see but a little space of sky—I will recall this day [traveling through the mountains of Switzerland on the way to Rome] and it will encourage me. I will make light of my own small troubles by thinking of the greatness and majesty of God.

Manuscript A

I resolved to give myself up more than ever to a serious and mortified life [during the three months Thérèse was forced to wait before she entered Carmel]. When I say mortified, I do not allude to the penances practiced by the saints. Far from resembling those heroic souls who from their childhood use fast and scourge and chain to discipline the flesh, I made my mortifications consist simply in checking my self-will, keeping back an impatient answer, rendering a small service in a quiet way, and a hundred other similar things.

Manuscript A

From illusions God in His mercy has ever preserved me. I found the religious life just what I had expected: sacrifice was never a matter of surprise....From the very outset my path was strewn with thorns rather than with roses.

Manuscript A

Suffering opened wide her arms to me from the first and I took her fondly to my heart. In the solemn examination before making the vows I declared my reasons for entering Carmel—"I have come to save souls and especially to pray for priests." The end cannot be reached without adopting the means, and since Our Lord had made me understand that it was through the cross He would give me souls, the more crosses I encountered the stronger became my attraction to suffering.

MANUSCRIPT A

I remember how in the month of June 1888, when we were afraid Papa might be stricken with cerebral paralysis, I surprised our Novice Mistress by saying, "I am suffering a great deal, Mother, yet I feel I can suffer still more." I did not then suspect the cross that awaited me. [Thérèse's father had developed cerebral arteriosclerosis.]

MANUSCRIPT A

*T*hough my suffering seemed to have reached its height, its attraction for me never lessened, and soon my soul shared in the trials the heart had to bear. My spiritual aridity increased, and I found no comfort in heaven or on earth. Yet amid these waters of tribulation so eagerly thirsted for, I was the happiest of mortals.

MANUSCRIPT A

*W*hen my heart, weary of the enveloping darkness, tries to find some rest and strength in the thought of an everlasting life to come, my anguish only increases. It seems to me that the darkness itself, borrowing the voice of the unbeliever, cries mockingly: "You dream of a land of light and fragrance, you believe that the Creator of these wonders will be forever yours, you think to escape one day from the mists in which you now languish. Hope on!…Look forward to death! It will give you, not what you hope for, but a night darker still, the night of utter nothingness!"

MANUSCRIPT B

*I*s there a greater joy than to suffer for Your love, O my God? The more intense and more hidden the suffering the more You value it.

MANUSCRIPT B

$\mathcal{M}$y whole strength lies in prayer and sacrifice: these are my invincible weapons, and experience has taught me that the heart is won by them rather than by words.

MANUSCRIPT B

$\mathcal{D}$o not think that I am overwhelmed with consolations. Far from it! My joy consists in being deprived of all joy here on earth. Jesus does not guide me openly; I neither see nor hear Him.

MANUSCRIPT C

$\mathcal{M}$artyrdom was the dream of my youth, and the dream has only grown more vivid in Carmel's narrow cell. Yet this too is folly, since to slake my thirst for suffering, not one, but every kind of torture would be needed.

MANUSCRIPT C

$\mathcal{U}$p to the age of fourteen, I practiced virtue without tasting its sweetness. I desired suffering, but I did not think of making it my joy; that grace was given to me later.

COUNSELS

$\mathcal{I}$f it be God's will that throughout your whole life you should feel a repugnance to suffering and humiliation—if He permits all the flowers of your desires and of your good will to fall to the ground without any fruit appearing, do not worry. At the hour of death, in the twinkling of an eye, He will cause rich fruits to ripen on the tree of your soul.

COUNSELS

$\mathcal{W}$hile in the world I used, on waking, to think of all the pleasant or unpleasant things that might happen throughout the day, and if I foresaw nothing but worries I got up with a heavy heart. Now it is the other way around. I think of the pains and of the sufferings awaiting me, and I rise, feeling all the more courageous and light of heart in proportion to the opportunities I foresee of proving my love for Our Lord.

COUNSELS

$\mathcal{S}$aints who suffer do not excite my pity. I know they have strength to bear their sufferings, and that through them they are giving great glory to God. But I have compassion for those who are not saints, and who do not know how to profit by suffering.

COUNSELS

There are people who make the worst of everything. With me it is different. I always see the good side of things. Even if it is my lot to suffer without a ray of comfort, well, I make that my joy.

COUNSELS

He [Jesus] is by our side, watching us and begging these tears. He needs them for our souls and the souls of others. I assure you that it costs Him dearly to fill us with bitterness, but He knows it is the only means of preparing us to know Him. [Letter to her biological sister Céline, who at the Lisieux Carmel assumed the name Sister Genevieve of the Holy Face.]

LETTER TO SISTER GENEVIEVE

Our martyrdom is beginning....Let us go forth to suffer together, dear sister, and let us offer our sufferings to Jesus for the salvation of souls.

LETTER TO SISTER GENEVIEVE

I must forget this world. Here everything wearies me—I find only one joy, that of suffering, and this joy, which is not a pleasure of the senses, is above all joy.

LETTER TO SISTER GENEVIEVE

The burden of our song is suffering, for Jesus offers us a chalice of great bitterness. Let us not withdraw our lips from it, but suffer in peace.

LETTER TO SISTER GENEVIEVE

Do not think that we can find love without suffering, for our nature remains and must be taken into account; but suffering puts great treasures within reach.

LETTER TO SISTER GENEVIEVE

We should like to suffer generously and nobly; we should like never to fall. What an illusion! What does it matter if I fall at every moment! In that way, I realize my weakness, and the gain is considerable.

LETTER TO SISTER GENEVIEVE

Today's trial [Thérèse's profession as a Carmelite] is one of those sorrows that are difficult to understand: a joy is set before me, one most natural and easy of attainment. I stretched forth my hands…and the coveted joy was withdrawn. But it is not the hand of humans that has done this thing—it is God's work.

LETTER TO SISTER GENEVIEVE

*Th*ree years ago our hearts had not yet been bruised, and life was one glad smile. Then Jesus looked down upon us, and all things were changed into an ocean of tears...but likewise into an ocean of grace and love.

We share the chalice of His [Jesus'] sufferings; but how sweet it will be to us one day to hear... "You are those who have stood by me in my trials, and I confer on you, just as my Father has conferred on me, a kingdom" (Luke 22:28–29).

What happiness it is to suffer for Him who loves us even unto folly, and to pass for fools in the eyes of the world.

You are right when you tell me that every cup must contain its drop of gall. I find that trials are a great help towards detachment from the things of earth. They make us look higher than this world. [Letter to her biological sister Pauline, who became prioress and was known as Mother Agnes of Jesus.]

I have a longing for those heart-wounds, those pin-pricks which inflict so much pain. I know of no ecstasy to which I do not prefer sacrifice. There I find happiness, and there alone.

LETTER TO MOTHER AGNES OF JESUS

I give thanks to Jesus for making me walk in darkness, and in the darkness I enjoy profound peace. Indeed, I consent to remain through all my religious life in the gloomy passage into which He has led me. I desire only that my darkness may obtain light for sinners. I am content, nay, full of joy, to be without all consolation.

LETTER TO MOTHER AGNES OF JESUS

*J*esus has visited us, and has found us worthy to be tried in the crucible of suffering. God has said that on the last day "He will wipe away all tears from our eyes" (Revelations 21:4), and no doubt that the more tears there are to dry, the greater will be the happiness. [Letter to her biological sister Marie, who took the name Sister Mary of the Sacred Heart.]

LETTER TO SISTER MARY OF
THE SACRED HEART

I thirst after heaven—that blessed home where our love for Jesus will be without bounds. True, we must pass through suffering and tears to reach that home, but I wish to suffer all that my Beloved is pleased to send me; I wish to let Him do as He wills with His "little ball" [Thérèse].

LETTER TO SISTER MARY
OF THE SACRED HEART

*I*n this world there is no fruitfulness without suffering—either physical pain, anguish of soul, or trials known sometimes only to God.

LAST WORDS

*W*hen Our Lord will have us suffer, there can be no evading it. For instance, when Sister Mary of the Sacred Heart was procuratrix she looked after me with a mother's tenderness. To all appearances I was pampered, and yet endless were the mortifications she imposed on me by serving me according to her own taste which was entirely different from mine.

LAST WORDS

*T*hroughout my religious life the cold has caused me more physical pain than anything else—I have suffered from cold until I almost died of it. [Thérèse made this admission when she was close to death.]

LAST WORDS

*D*o you see this little glass? One would suppose it contained a most delicious drink, whereas in reality it is more bitter than anything I take. It is the image of my life. To others it has been all rose-colored; they imagine that I have drunk of a most delicious wine, but to me it has been full of bitterness. I say bitterness, yet, after all, my life has not been sad, because I have learned to find joy and sweetness in all that is bitter.

LAST WORDS

I can no longer suffer, because all suffering is sweet. Besides it is a great mistake to worry as to what trouble there may be in store; it is like meddling with God's work.

LAST WORDS

The devil is beside me. I do not see him but I feel him; he torments me, holding me with a grip of iron that I may not find one crumb of comfort, and adding to my sufferings that I may be driven to despair....Something mysterious is happening within me. I am not suffering for myself but for some other soul, and Satan is angry. [Suffering from tuberculosis, Thérèse spoke these words in asking the infirmarian to sprinkle her bed with holy water.]

LAST WORDS

I have always forced myself to love suffering and to welcome it gladly. When I suffer much, when painful and disagreeable things come my way, instead of looking sad I greet them with a smile. At first I did not always succeed, but now it has become a habit which I am truly glad to have acquired.

LAST WORDS

All that I have written of my thirst for suffering is really true. I have no regret for having surrendered myself to Love.

SPOKEN SHORTLY BEFORE HER DEATH

$\mathcal{A}$BANDONED TO
THE WILL OF GOD

Abandoned to the Will of God

Abandonment to the will of God the North Star that guided Thérèse through the pathways of the world. She gave herself over to carrying out God's will for the sake of her love for him. Thérèse was supremely confident in God's mercy and generosity and was truly dedicated to doing his will in the little trifles of life. Thérèse had no desire except to rest in the arms of her heavenly Father. She desired to leave the choice of everything in her life to him.

Our Lord has been pleased to create great saints who may be compared to the lily and the rose; but He has also created lesser ones, who must be content to be daisies or simple violets flowering at His feet, and whose mission is to gladden His divine eyes when He deigns to look down on them: the more joyfully they do His will, the greater is their perfection.

MANUSCRIPT A

Saint Cecilia became my chosen patroness as well as the keeper of my most intimate thoughts, for what appealed to me above all else was her perfect abandonment to God and her unbounded confidence in Him.

MANUSCRIPT A

It was brought home to me one day during prayer that my too eager desire to take my vows was mingled with much self-love. Since I belonged to Our Lord and was His little plaything to amuse and console Him, it was for me to do His will and not for Him to do mine.

MANUSCRIPT A

Far from feeling consoled, I went through the retreat before my profession in a state of utter spiritual desolation—seemingly abandoned by God....Yet apparently barren as was my retreat, I received unconsciously many interior lights on the best means of pleasing God. I have often observed that Our Lord will never give me a store of provisions, but nourishes me at each moment with food that is always new. I find it within my soul without knowing how it has come. I believe, quite simply, that it is Jesus Himself, hidden in my poor heart, who is mysteriously at work inspiring me from hour to hour with whatever He wishes me to do.

MANUSCRIPT A

I have no further desire unless it is to love Jesus even unto folly! … Already I have suffered much; already it has seemed to me that my small boat was nearing the Eternal Shore. From my earliest years I believed the Little Flower would be gathered in her springtime, but now the spirit of self-abandonment is my sole guide.

MANUSCRIPT A

I shall not recover from this sickness. My soul, nevertheless, abides in peace, for I have long since ceased to belong to myself. I have surrendered my whole being to my Spouse, and He is free to do with me whatsoever He chooses.

MANUSCRIPT A

The knowledge that it was impossible to do anything of myself greatly simplified my task [as novice mistress], and confident that the rest would be given me over and above, the one aim of my interior life was to unite myself more and more closely with God.

MANUSCRIPT B

*I*n the abstract it seems easy to do good to souls, to make them love God more, and to mold them to one's own ideas. But, when we put our hands to the work, we quickly learn that without God's help it is as impossible to do good to them, as to bring back the sun once it has set.

MANUSCRIPT B

O Jesus! I would like to tell all the little souls of Your ineffable condescension! If by any possibility You could find a soul weaker than mine, one that should abandon itself with perfect trust to Your Infinite Mercy, I feel that You would take delight in loading that soul with still greater favors.

MANUSCRIPT C

*T*hough from the age of three I have never refused Almighty God anything, still I cannot boast. See how this evening the tree-tops are gilded by the setting sun. So likewise my soul appears to you all shining and golden because it is exposed to the rays of Love. But should the divine Sun no longer shine, it would instantly be sunk in gloom.

COUNSELS

55

The smallest act of self-denial is worth more than the writing of pious books or of beautiful poems. When we feel keenly how incapable we are of doing anything worthwhile, the best remedy is to offer to God the good works of others.

COUNSELS

If only we could realize what we gain by self-denial in all things....I have tried not to seek myself in anything.

COUNSELS

To be a true victim of love we must surrender ourselves entirely....Love will consume us only in the measure of our self-surrender.

COUNSELS

God will do all I wish in heaven, because I have never done my own will on earth.

COUNSELS

I never lose courage. I leave myself in the arms of Our Lord. He teaches me "to draw profit from everything, from the good and from the bad which He finds in me" (Saint John of the Cross). He teaches me to speculate in the bank of love, or rather it is He who speculates for me, without telling me how He does it—that is His affair, not mine. I have but to surrender myself wholly to Him, to do so without reserve, without even the satisfaction of knowing what it is all bringing to me.

Mother, if you knew how utterly indifferent to earthly things I desire to be, and of how little concern to me are all the beauties of creation! I should be wretched if I possessed them. My heart seems so vast when I think of the goods of the earth—all of them together unable to fill it. But by the side of Jesus it looks so small.

Innumerable roads spread out before my gaze, but so many of these were perfect that I felt incapable of choosing any of my own free will. Then I said to my Divine Guide: "You know where I should go…and for whose sake I would climb this Mountain. You know who possesses the love of my heart. For Him alone I set out on the journey; lead me therefore by the paths of His choosing."

The glory of Jesus—this is my sole ambition. I abandon my glory to Him; and if He seems to forget me, well, He is free to do so since I am no longer my own, but His. He will weary sooner of making me wait than I shall of waiting.

LETTER TO MOTHER AGNES OF JESUS

I believe that the work of Jesus has been to detach me from everything but Himself. My only comfort is the exceeding strength and peace that is mine. I hope to be just what He wills I should be, and in this lies all my happiness.

LETTER TO SISTER MARY OF THE SACRED HEART

I know that many saints have passed their lives in the practice of amazing penance. But what of that? "In my father's house there are many mansions" (John 14:2). These are the words of Jesus, and therefore I follow the path He marks out for me; I try to be in no way concerned about myself, and to abandon unreservedly to Him the work He deigns to accomplish in my soul.

LETTER TO A MISSIONARY PRIEST

All I desire is God's holy will, and if in heaven I could no longer work for His glory, I should prefer exile to home.

LETTER TO A MISSIONARY PRIEST

I feel we must tread the same road to heaven, the road of suffering and love. When I myself have reached the port, I will teach you how best to sail the world's tempestuous sea— with the self-abandonment of a child well aware of its father's love, and of his vigilance in the hour of danger.

LETTER TO A MISSIONARY PRIEST

I turn to God and to all of His saints and I thank them notwithstanding [for the feelings of being discouraged and forsaken]; I believe they want to see how far I will trust them. But the words of Job have not entered my heart in vain: "Even if God should kill me, I would still trust Him" (Job 13:15). I admit that it has taken a long time to arrive at this degree of self-abandonment; but I have reached it now, and it is Our Lord Himself who has brought me there.

LAST WORDS

Our Lord's will fills my heart to the brim, and if anything else be added, it cannot penetrate to any depth, but, like oil on the surface of limpid waters, glides easily across. If my heart were not already brimming over, if it needed to be filled by the feelings of joy and sadness that follow each other so rapidly, then indeed it would be flooded by bitter sorrow; but these quick-succeeding changes scarcely ruffle the surface of my soul, and in its depths there reigns a peace that nothing can disturb.

LAST WORDS

I desire neither death nor life. Were Our Lord to offer me my choice, I would not choose. I only will what He wills, and I am pleased with whatever He does. I have no fear of the last struggle, or of any pain, however great, which my illness may bring. God has always been my help; He has led me by the hand since I was a child and I count on Him now. Even though suffering should reach its furthest limits I am certain He will never forsake me.

LAST WORDS

DEVOTED TO LOVE OF GOD

Devoted to Love of God

*In the life of Saint Thérèse of Lisieux, love of God played
a central part. This love provided the energy that enriched
her spiritual life and was the uppermost goal of her "little
way." Thérèse saw her love of God as the only appropri-
ate response to God's immeasurable love for her. The Little Flower's whole life was one long canticle of love, and it
was the transforming focus of her path to God. Her desire
to be perfect even in her smallest actions, her love of suffering, her zeal for the salvation of souls, and her focus on
being united with Jesus above all others give an indication
of the depth and extent of Thérèse's love.*

Even though I had been long thinking of
my first Communion, I must stir up in my heart
fresh transports of love and fill it with flowers.
Every day, therefore, I made a number of little
sacrifices and acts of love which were to be
transformed into so many flowers: violets or
roses, cornflowers, daisies, or forget-me-nots—
in a word, all nature's blossoms were to form
within me a cradle for the Holy Child.

MANUSCRIPT A

*H*ow sweet was the first embrace of Jesus [at Thérèse's first Communion]. It was indeed an embrace of love. I felt that I was loved, and said: "I love You, and I give myself to You for ever."

MANUSCRIPT A

*M*y Father wishes me to love Him because He has forgiven me, not much, but everything. Without waiting for me to love Him much as Saint Mary Magdalen did, He has made me understand how He has loved me with an ineffable love and forethought, in order that my own love may reach even unto folly.

MANUSCRIPT A

*O*ne evening, not knowing in what words to tell Jesus how much I loved Him, and how much I wished that He might be everywhere honored and served, the sad thought forced itself upon my mind that from the depths of hell there would never go up to Him one single act of love. I then cried out that I would gladly be cast into that place of torment and blasphemy to make Him eternally loved even there. Of course, this could not be for His glory, since He desires only our happiness, but love needs to speak foolishly.

MANUSCRIPT A

I, who never yet had to speak except to answer questions addressed to me, would have to explain and enlarge on my reasons for wishing to enter Carmel. It cost me a great effort to overcome my shyness sufficiently for this, yet it is true that love knows no such word as "impossible," but believes "it may and can do all things." I had to purchase my happiness by heavy trials, and nothing but the love of Jesus could have made me face these hardships. [Here Thérèse reflects on a meeting with the bishop of Bayeux, France.]

MANUSCRIPT A

I had long felt that Our Lord is more tender than a mother....I know, by sweet experience, how ready a mother is to forgive the involuntary small faults of her child, and I remember how no reproach could have touched me more than one single kiss from you [Pauline, Thérèse's sister]. Fear makes me shrink, while under love's sweet rule I not only advance—I fly.

MANUSCRIPT A

*E*xperience taught me that the sole happiness of this earth consists in being hidden and remaining in total ignorance of created things. I understood that without love, even the most brilliant deeds count for nothing.

MANUSCRIPT A

*H*ow sweet is the way of Love! True, one may fall and be unfaithful to grace, but Love knows how to draw profit from everything, and quickly consumes whatever may be displeasing to Our Lord, leaving in the heart only a deep and humble peace.

MANUSCRIPT A

*O*n every side Your Merciful Love is ignored and rejected....Those hearts on which You would lavish it turn to creatures and seek their happiness in the miserable satisfaction of a moment, rather than cast themselves into Your arms—into the ecstatic fires of Your infinite Love.

MANUSCRIPT A

$\mathcal{M}$y God, it seems to me that if You would find souls offering themselves as a holocaust to Your Love, You would consume them rapidly and would be pleased to set free those flames of infinite tenderness now imprisoned in Your heart.

MANUSCRIPT A

$\mathcal{O}$ my Jesus! You never ask what is impossible; You know better than I how frail and imperfect I am; You know that I shall never love my Sisters [in Carmel] as You have loved them, unless You love them Yourself within me. It is because You desire to grant me this grace that You have given a new Commandment, and dearly do I cherish it, since it proves to me that it is Your will to love in me all those You bid me to love.

MANUSCRIPT B

$\mathcal{W}$hen I show charity towards others, I know that it is Jesus who is acting within me, and the more closely I am united to Him, the more dearly I love my Sisters. Should I wish to increase this love, and should the devil bring before me the defects of a Sister, I hasten to look for her virtues and good motives.

MANUSCRIPT B

*M*y God, You know that I have always desired to love You alone. I seek no other glory. Your love has gone before me from the days of my childhood. It has grown with my growth, and now it is an abyss, the depth of which I cannot sound.

MANUSCRIPT B

*L*ove attracts love, and mine, as it darts toward You, my God, wishes to fill to the brim the Abyss that draws it, but alas! My love is not even a drop in that Ocean. To love You as You love me, I must borrow Your own love—thus only can my desire be satisfied.

MANUSCRIPT B

I ask Jesus to draw me into the fire of His Love, and to unite me so closely to Himself that He may live and act in me. I feel that the more the fire of love consumes my heart,...the more also will those souls who come in contact with mine "run swiftly in the sweet odor of the Beloved."

MANUSCRIPT B

*J*esus deigns to point out to me the only way …to Love's divine furnace, and that way is self-surrender: it is the confidence of the little child who sleeps without fear in its father's arms.

MANUSCRIPT C

If all weak and imperfect souls such as mine felt as I do, none would despair of reaching the summit of the mountain of Love, since Jesus does not look for deeds, but only for gratitude and self-surrender.

MANUSCRIPT C

I understood that since the Church is a body composed of different members, she could not lack the most necessary and most nobly endowed of all the bodily organs. I understood, therefore, that the Church has a heart—and a heart on fire with love. I saw, too, that love alone imparts life to all the members, so that should love ever fail, apostles would no longer preach the Gospel and martyrs would refuse to shed their blood. Finally, I realized that love includes every vocation, that love is all things, that love is eternal, reaching down through the ages and stretching to the uttermost limits of earth.

MANUSCRIPT C

This is all Our Lord claims of us. He needs our love; He has no need of our works. True, the same God who declares He has no need to tell us if He is hungry, did not disdain to beg a little water from the Samaritan woman: but when He said "Give me to drink," He was asking for the love of His creatures. He thirsted, indeed, but He thirsted for love.

MANUSCRIPT C

I cried out: "O Jesus, my Love, my vocation is found at last—my vocation is love!" I have found my place in the bosom of the Church, and this place, O my God, You have Yourself given to me: in the heart of the Church, I will be love!

MANUSCRIPT C

I am but a weak and helpless child, but my very weakness makes me dare to offer myself, O Jesus, as victim to Your Love. In older days, only pure and spotless holocausts would be accepted by God, nor could His Justice be appeased except by the most perfect sacrifices; but now that the law of fear has given way to the law of love, I have been chosen, though a weak and imperfect creature, as Love's victim.

MANUSCRIPT C

$\mathcal{L}$ove is repaid by Love alone" [motto of Saint Teresa of Ávila]. Well do I know it, my God! And therefore I have sought and have found a way to ease my heart by giving You love for love.

MANUSCRIPT C

$\mathcal{O}$ne thought is mine from now on, dear Jesus, it is to love You! Great deeds are forbidden me. I can neither preach the Gospel nor shed my blood…but what does it matter! My brothers labor in my stead while I, a little child, stay close to the Throne and love You for all those who are in the strife.

MANUSCRIPT C

$\mathcal{H}$ow can a soul so imperfect as mine aspire to the plenitude of Love? What is the key to this mystery? O my only Friend!—why do You not reserve these infinite longings for lofty souls, for the eagles that soar in the heights? Alas! I am only a little unfledged bird. Yet the eagle's spirit is mine, and notwithstanding my littleness I dare to gaze upon the Divine Sun of Love.

MANUSCRIPT C

$\mathcal{I}$ know well that for Your sake the saints have made themselves foolish—being "eagles" they have done great things. Too little for such mighty deeds, my folly lies in the hope that Your Love accepts me as a victim, and in my confidence that the angels and saints will help me to fly unto You with Your own wings, O my Divine Eagle. As long as You will it, I will remain with my gaze fixed upon You, for I long to be fascinated by Your divine eyes, I long to become Love's prey. I am filled with the hope that one day You will swoop down upon me, and bearing me away to the source of all Love, will plunge me at last into its glowing abyss.

MANUSCRIPT C

$\mathcal{M}$y special favorites in heaven are those who, so to speak, stole it, such as the Holy Innocents and the Good Thief. There are great saints who won it by their works. I want to be like the thieves and to win it by stratagem—a stratagem of love which will open its gates to me and to poor sinners.

COUNSELS

71

*D*o not fear to tell Jesus that you love Him, even though you may not actually feel that love. In this way, you will compel Him to come to you, and carry you like a little child who is too weak to walk.

Counsels

*T*ears for God will never do. Far less to Him than to His creatures ought you to show a mournful face. He comes to our cloisters in search of rest—to forget the unceasing complaints of His friends in the world, who, instead of appreciating the value of the Cross, receive it more often than not with moans and tears. Frankly, this is not disinterested love....It is for us to console Our Lord, and not for Him to be always consoling us.

Counsels

*O*ur Lord is justice itself, and if He does not judge our good actions, neither will He judge our bad ones. It seems to me that for victims of love there will be no judgment. God will rather hasten to reward with eternal delights His own love which He will behold burning in their hearts.

Counsels

It would not disturb me (supposing the impossible) if God Himself did not see my good actions. I love Him so much that I would like to give Him joy without His knowing who gave it. When He does know, He is, as it were, obliged to make a return. I should not like to give Him the trouble.

COUNSELS

When in the morning, we feel no courage or strength for the practice of virtue, it is really a grace: it is time to rely on Jesus alone. If we fall, an act of love will set all right, and Jesus smiles. He helps us without seeming to do so; and the tears which sinners cause Him to shed are wiped away by our feeble love. Love can do all things. The most impossible tasks seem to it easy and sweet.

LETTER TO SISTER GENEVIEVE

I know that by humiliation alone saints can be made, and I also know that our trial is a mine of gold for us to turn to account. I am but a little grain of sand, yet I wish to set to work, though I have neither courage nor strength. But my very weakness will make my task easier, for I wish to work for love.

LETTER TO SISTER GENEVIEVE

There is but one thing to be done here below: to love Jesus, and to save souls for Him that He may be more loved. We must not let slip the smallest opportunity of giving Him joy. We must refuse Him nothing. He is in such need of love.

LETTER TO SISTER GENEVIEVE

To keep the word of Jesus is the one condition of our happiness, the proof of our love for Him; and this word seems to me to be His very Self, for He calls Himself the uncreated Word of the Father.

LETTER TO SISTER GENEVIEVE

I do not wish creatures to have one atom of my love. I wish to give all to Jesus, since He makes me understand that He alone is perfect happiness….And even when I have nothing, as is the case tonight, I will give Him this nothing.

LETTER TO MOTHER AGNES OF JESUS

Love can take the place of a long life. Jesus does not consider time, for He is eternal. He looks only at the love.

LETTER TO MOTHER AGNES OF JESUS

*H*ere is the dream of this "grain of sand" [metaphor for Thérèse herself]. Love Jesus alone, and nothing else beside! The grain of sand is so small that if it wished to open its heart to any other but Jesus, there would no longer be room for this Beloved.

LETTER TO MOTHER AGNES OF JESUS

*L*et us learn to keep this God prisoner— the Divine Beggar of Love. By telling us that a single hair can work this wonder, He shows us that the smallest actions done for His love are those which charm His heart.

LETTER TO SISTER FRANCES TERESA

*Y*ou ask me for a method of attaining perfection. I know of Love—and Love only! Our hearts are made for it alone. [From a letter to Thérèse's aunt Marie Guérin who became Sister Marie-Dosithée.]

LETTER TO SISTER MARIE-DOSITHÉE

$\mathcal{S}$ince I have been given to understand the love of the Heart of Jesus, I confess that all fear has been driven from mine. The remembrance of my faults humbles me, and helps me never to rely on my own strength, which is mere weakness. More than all, it speaks to me of mercy and of love. When a soul with childlike trust casts her faults into Love's all-devouring furnace, how can they escape being utterly consumed?

LETTER TO A MISSIONARY PRIEST

$\mathcal{I}$t is a great mistake to worry as to what trouble there may be in store; it is like meddling with God's work. We who run in the way of Love must never allow ourselves to be disturbed by anything. If I did not simply suffer from one moment to another, it would be impossible for me to be patient; but I look only at the present, I forget the past, and I take good care not to forestall the future.

LAST WORDS

$\mathcal{O}$ my God, I love You.

THÉRÈSE'S LAST WORDS

HUMBLY HIDDEN
IN THE HEART
OF GOD

Humbly Hidden in the Heart of God

Humility is the virtue that puts us in our correct place as a child before God and asks us to acknowledge our faults, weaknesses, and imperfections to God, to ourselves, and to others. Saint Thérèse of Lisieux was a master practitioner of humility, and many of her sufferings and humiliations were hidden ones. She willingly remained humble in the face of many unforgiving tests of her vocation and love of God. Her prioress reproached her frequently, saying such things as "It is easy to see that our cloisters are swept by a child of fifteen!" and "What is this that a novice has to be sent for a walk every day!" Even at the end of her life, a comment expressed by a sister at recreation was reported to her. She had said: "I don't know why they talk about Sister Thérèse as if she were a saint. It is true she had practiced virtue, but it is not a virtue she acquired through humiliations and sufferings." "And I," confessed Thérèse, "when I recall how much I have suffered from my early years! How profitable it is to learn what others think of me when I am about to die!" Thérèse's teachings show us how a true understanding of humility is a firm foundation for our own spiritual life.

*T*he more crosses I encountered, the stronger became my attraction to suffering. Unknown to anyone, this was the path I trod for fully five years: it was precisely the flower I wished to offer to Jesus—a hidden flower which keeps its perfume only for heaven.

MANUSCRIPT A

I had not appreciated the beauties of the Holy Face until you, my little Mother, unveiled them to me. You were the first to penetrate the mysteries of the love hidden in the Face of our Divine Spouse....More than ever it came home to me in what true glory consists. He whose "kingdom is not of this world" (John 17:36) taught me that the only kingdom worth coveting is the grace of being unknown and esteemed as nothing, and the joy that comes of self-contempt. I wished that, like the Face of Jesus, mine "should be, as it were, hidden and despised" (Isaiah 53:3), so that no one on earth should esteem me: I thirsted to suffer and to be forgotten.

MANUSCRIPT A

$\mathcal{I}$ endeavored, above all, to practice little hidden acts of virtue, such as folding the mantles which the sisters had forgotten and being on the alert to render them help.

MANUSCRIPT A

$\mathcal{Y}$ou, Reverend Mother, did not consider it imprudent to assure me one day that the Divine Master was enlightening me and giving me the experience of years. I am now too little to be guilty of vanity, and too little to try to prove my humility by high-sounding words. I prefer, therefore, to own in all simplicity that "He who is mighty has done great things to me" (Luke 1:49), and the greatest of all is that He has shown me my littleness and how of myself I am incapable of anything good.

MANUSCRIPT B

$\mathcal{D}$ear Jesus, for the love of You, your child will sit at the table of bitterness where these poor sinners take their food and will not rise from it until You have given the sign. But may she not say in her own name and in the name of her guilty brethren: "O God, be merciful to us sinners" (Luke 18:13).

MANUSCRIPT B

$\mathcal{I}$ know only too well of how little use I am, and it would not be for the sake of the service I might render to the Carmel of Hanoi that I would leave everything dear to me; my sole reason would be to do God's Will and to sacrifice myself for Him at His good pleasure.

MANUSCRIPT B

$\mathcal{I}$t may be that at some future day my present state will appear to me full of defects, but nothing now surprises me. Nor does my utter helplessness distress me; I even glory in it, and expect each day to reveal some imperfection.

MANUSCRIPT B

$\mathcal{H}$ow glad I am that from the beginning I learned to practice self-denial! Already I enjoyed the reward promised to those who fight bravely, and I no longer feel the need of refusing all consolation to my heart, for my heart is set on God. Because it has loved only Him, it has grown little by little, till it can give to those who are dear to Him a far deeper love than if it were centered in a barren and selfish affection.

MANUSCRIPT B

I cannot say that Our Lord makes me walk in the way of exterior humiliation; He is content with humbling me in my inmost soul....At the moment when I least expect it, lifting the veil that hides my faults, God allows my novices to see me as I really am and they do not find me altogether to their liking. With a simplicity that is delightful, they tell me how I try them and what they dislike in me; in fact they are as frank as through it were a question of someone else.

MANUSCRIPT B

*H*ow shall I show my love, since love proves itself by deeds? I, the little one, will strew flowers, perfuming the Divine Throne with their fragrance. I will sing Love's canticle in silvery tones...To strew flowers is the only means of proving my love, and these flowers will be each word and look, each little daily sacrifice.

MANUSCRIPT B

*A*ll my life long He has done that for me—He has completely hidden me under His wing. [Stated by Thérèse upon seeing a little white hen sheltering its chicks under its wings.]

MANUSCRIPT B

*W*hy try to overcome temptations. Rather try to undergo them. It is all very well for great souls to soar above the clouds when the storm bursts. We have simply to stand in the rain. What does it matter if we get wet? We can dry ourselves in the sunshine of love.

COUNSELS

*W*e keep little when we recognize our own nothingness and expect everything from the goodness of God, exactly as a little child expects everything from his father.

COUNSELS

*I*t is Jesus who takes it upon Himself to fill your soul accordingly as you rid it of imperfections. I see clearly that you are mistaking the road, and that you will never arrive at the end of your journey. You want to climb up the mountain, whereas God wishes you to climb down. He is awaiting you below in the fruitful valley of humility. [Thérèse's advice to a young novice.]

COUNSELS

To me it seems that humility is truth. I do not know whether I am humble, but I do know that I see the truth in all things.

COUNSELS

You must practice the little virtues. This is sometimes difficult, but God never refuses the first grace—courage for self-conquest; and if the soul corresponds to that grace, she at once finds herself in God's sunlight.

COUNSELS

To believe oneself imperfect and others perfect—this is true happiness. Should earthly creatures think you wanting in virtue, they rob you of nothing, and you are none the poorer: it is they who lose.

COUNSELS

Honors are always dangerous. What poisonous food is served daily to those in high positions! What deadly fumes of incense! A soul must be well detached from herself to pass unscathed through it all.

COUNSELS

$\mathcal{I}$ was watching the flicker of a tiny night light. One of the Sisters came up and, having lit her own candle in the dying flame, passed it round to light the candles of the others. And the thought came to me: "Who dare glory in their own good works?" It needs but one such faint spark to set the whole world on fire. We come in touch with burning and shining lights, set high on the candlestick of the Church, and we think we are receiving from them grace and light. But from where do they borrow their fire? Very possibly from the prayers of some devout and hidden soul whose inward shining is not apparent to human eyes.

COUNSELS

$\mathcal{T}$he great saints themselves, seeing what they owe to us little souls, will love us with a love beyond compare. Friendship in Paradise will be both sweet and full of surprises. A shepherd boy may be the familiar friend of an apostle or of a great Doctor of the Church, a little child may be in close intimacy with a Patriarch.

COUNSELS

The lowest place is the only spot on earth which is not open to envy. Here alone there is neither vanity nor affliction of spirit. Yet "the way of man is not his own" (Jeremiah 10:23), and sometimes we find ourselves wishing for the things that dazzle. When that happens, there is nothing for it but to take our stand among the imperfect and look upon ourselves as very little souls who at every instant need to be upheld by the goodness of God. He reaches out His hand to us, the very moment He sees us fully convinced of our nothingness....Should we attempt great things, however, even under the pretext of zeal, He deserts us. So all we have to do is to humble ourselves, to bear with meekness our imperfections. Herein lies—for us—true holiness.

Counsels

Compare this little act of virtue with what Our Lord has the right to expect of you! Rather you should humble yourself for having lost so many opportunities of proving your love.

Counsels

$\mathcal{M}$y God, permit that I may be rebuked by those just souls who surround me. I ask also that the oil of praise, so sweet to our nature, may not perfume my head, that is to say, my mind, by making me believe that I possess virtues when I have merely performed a few good actions.

"Jesus!" Your name is as oil poured out, and it is in this divine perfume that I desire wholly to hide myself from all worldly eyes.

COUNSELS

$\mathcal{G}$od does not despise these hidden struggles within ourselves, so much richer in merit because they are unseen: "The patient man is better than the valiant, and he that rules his spirit is better than one who takes cities" (Proverbs 26:32). Through our little acts of charity, practiced in the dark, as it were, we obtain the conversion of the godless, help missionaries, and gain for them plentiful alms.

COUNSELS

*H*appy dew drop, known to God alone, pay no heed to the roaring torrents of the world! Do not envy the crystal stream which winds among the meadows. The ripple of its waters may be most sweet, but it can be heard by creatures. Besides, the field-flower could never contain it in its cup. One must be so lowly to draw near to Jesus, and few are the souls that aspire to be lowly and unknown.

LETTER TO SISTER GENEVIEVE

*W*hat happiness to be so entirely hidden that no one gives us a thought—to be unknown even to those with whom we live! My little Mother, I long to be unknown to every one of God's creatures! I have never desired glory among men, and if their contempt formerly attracted my heart, I have realized that even that is too glorious for me, and I thirst to be forgotten.

LETTER TO MOTHER AGNES OF JESUS

SECLUDED IN THE
LITTLE WAY

Secluded in the Little Way

The constant use of diminutives in the Martin household is, in a sense, prophetic of Thérèse's way of perfection: She was known as "the little Thérèse," "the little Queen," "the little lamb," "dearest little rogue," "little puss." However, this road to sanctity is far from a miniature achievement. Rather, Thérèse's little doctrine of love and lowliness is the summit of her path to holiness, her achievement of the fullness of God's mercy. Her goal to teach souls the gentleness of the Good Lord was realized by the publication of her autobiography. She felt that this doctrine came from God but, as a precaution, she announced to her novices that "if I lead you into error with my Little Way of Love, do not be afraid that I will permit you to follow it for any length of time. I would soon reappear after my death and tell you to take a different road." Even though Thérèse portrayed her little way as a short and straightforward method to attain salvation, its simplicity is belied by the difficult discipline of its implementation. Indeed, the little way is not a compromise with human weakness.

*O*n that day [Thérèse's first Communion day] our meeting was more than simple recognition, it was perfect union. We were no longer two. Thérèse had disappeared like a drop of water lost in the immensity of the ocean; Jesus alone remained—He was the Master, the King. Had not Thérèse asked Him to take away the liberty which frightened her? She felt herself so weak and frail that she wished to be forever united to the Divine Strength.

MANUSCRIPT A

*S*uppose that the father, knowing that a large stone lies on his son's path, anticipates the danger and, unseen by anyone, hastens to remove it. Unconscious of the accident from which such tender forethought has saved him, the son will not show any mark of gratitude for it, or feel the same love for his father as he would have done had he been cured of some grievous wound. But if he came to learn the whole truth, would he not love his father all the more?

Well now, I am this child, the object of the foreseeing love of a Father "who did not send His Son to call the just, but sinners" (Luke 5:32).

MANUSCRIPT A

$\mathcal{F}$or some time past I had offered myself to the Child Jesus to be His little plaything; I told Him not to treat me like one of those precious toys which children only look at and dare not touch, but rather as a little ball of no value that could be thrown on the ground, tossed about, pierced, left in a corner, or pressed to His heart, just as it might please Him. In a word, all I desired was to amuse the Holy Child, to let Him play with me just as it might please Him.

My prayer had been heard. In time, Jesus pierced His little plaything, anxious, no doubt, to see what it contained. Then, satisfied with what He found, He let the ball drop and went to sleep....Jesus dreamed that He was still at play; that He took up the ball, or threw it down, or else rolled it far away; but that finally He pressed it to His heart and never again allowed it to slip from His hand.

MANUSCRIPT A

$\mathcal{I}$ suppose I ought to be distressed that I so often fall asleep during meditation and thanksgiving after Holy Communion, but I reflect that little children, asleep or awake, are equally dear to their parents.

MANUSCRIPT A

I have always desired to become a saint, but in comparing myself with the saints I have ever felt that I am as far removed from them as a grain of sand....Instead of feeling discouraged by such reflections, I concluded that God would not inspire a wish which could not be realized, and that in spite of my littleness I might aim at being a saint. "It is impossible," I said, "for me to become great, so I must bear with myself and many imperfections, but I will seek out a means of reaching heaven by a little way—very short, very straight, and entirely new."

MANUSCRIPT B

*W*e live in an age of inventions: there are now elevators that save us the trouble of climbing stairs. I will try to find an elevator by which I may be raised unto God, for I am too small to climb the steep stairway of perfection.

MANUSCRIPT B

I sought to find in Holy Scripture some suggestion of what this desired elevator might be, and I came across those words: "Whosoever is a little one, let him come to me" (Proverbs 9:4). I therefore drew near to God, feeling sure I had discovered what I had sought.

MANUSCRIPT B

*F*rom the moment I entered the sanctuary of souls [as novice mistress], I saw at a glance that the task was beyond my strength, and quickly taking refuge in Our Lord's arms, I imitated those babes who when frightened hide their faces on their father's shoulder.

MANUSCRIPT B

*Y*ou see that I am but a very little soul who can offer to God only very little things. It still happens that I frequently miss the opportunity of welcoming these small sacrifices which bring so much peace; but I am not discouraged—I bear the loss of a little peace and I try to be more watchful in the future.

MANUSCRIPT B

*I*s there on earth a soul more feeble than mine? Yet precisely because of my feebleness You have been pleased to grant my least, my most childish desires.

MANUSCRIPT C

$\mathcal{I}$ was a child of light, and I understood that my desires of embracing every vocation were riches that might well make me unjust; so I employed them in the making of friends. I presented myself before the company of the angels and saints and spoke to them thus: "I am the least of all creatures, I know my worthlessness, but I also know how noble and generous hearts love to do good. Therefore, O blessed inhabitants of the Heavenly City, I entreat you to adopt me as your child. All the glory you may help me to acquire will be yours; condescend, then, to hear my prayer and obtain for me a double portion of your love for God."

I dare not try to understand all that my prayer means, O my God! I should fear to be crushed by the mere weight of its audacity. That I am Your child is my only excuse, for children do not grasp the full meaning of their words.

MANUSCRIPT C

*O*f what avail to You are my flowers and my songs, dear Jesus? I know well that this fragrant shower, these petals of little price, these songs of love from a poor little heart like mine, will nevertheless be pleasing to You....The Church Triumphant, stooping toward her child, will gather up these scattered rose leaves, and, placing them in Your divine hands, that they may acquire an infinite value, will shower them on the Church Suffering to extinguish the flames, and on the Church Militant to make her triumph.

MANUSCRIPT C

*S*uch a trifle would not have caused this if God had not wished to make me understand that the great austerities of the saints are not meant for me or for the little souls who are to walk by the same path of spiritual childhood. [Thérèse commenting on falling ill after wearing a sharply pointed iron cross that pierced her flesh.]

MANUSCRIPT C

*O*ne must keep little in order to make quick progress along the path of divine love. That is what I have done.

COUNSELS

$\mathcal{Y}$ou [a young novice] remind me of a little child just learning how to stand on its feet, yet determined to climb a flight of stairs in order to find its mother. Time after time it tries to set its tiny foot upon the lowest step, and each time it stumbles and falls. Do as that little one did. By the practice of all the virtues keep on lifting your foot to climb the ladder of perfection, but do not imagine you can yourself succeed in mounting even the very first step. God asks of you nothing but goodwill. From the top of the ladder He looks down lovingly; and, presently, touched by your fruitless efforts, He will take you in His arms to His kingdom, never to be parted from Him again. But if you leave off lifting your foot, your stay on the ground will indeed be a long one.

COUNSELS

$\mathcal{B}$eing as a little child with God means that we do not attribute to ourselves the virtues we may possess, in the belief that we are capable of something. It implies, on the contrary, our recognition of the fact that God places the treasure of virtue in the hand of His little child for him to use as he needs it, though all the while it is God's treasure.

COUNSELS

When we keep little we recognize our own nothingness and expect everything from the goodness of God, exactly as a little child expects everything from its father. Nothing worries us, not even the amassing of spiritual riches.

Even among the very poor a little child is always given what he needs. Once, however, he is grown up, his father will no longer feed him, but tells him to find work and earn his living. Well, I do not want to hear my Heavenly Father talk like this to me, and so I have never wished to grow up. I feel incapable of earning my livelihood—of earning Life Eternal. And so I have always tried to be as a little child, occupied merely in gathering flowers of love and sacrifice with which to please Almighty God. [Thérèse responding when asked what must be done to be "as little children."]

COUNSELS

To keep little means not to lose courage at the sight of our faults. Little children often tumble, but they are too small to suffer grievous injury.

COUNSELS

*B*e of good courage. In heaven nothing will look black, everything will be dazzling white, bathed in the divine radiance of Our Spouse, the pure white Lily of the Valley. Together we will follow Him wherever he goes. Meanwhile we must make good use of our life here below. Let us give Our Lord pleasure, let us by self-sacrifice give Him souls! Above all, let us be little, so little that everyone may tread us underfoot, without our even seeming to suffer pain.

COUNSELS

I am not a saint. I have never wrought the works of a saint. I am but a tiny soul whom Almighty God has loaded with His favors.

COUNSELS

I often compare myself to a little bowl filled by God with good things. All the kittens come to eat from it, and they sometimes quarrel as to which will have the largest share. But the Holy Child Jesus keeps a sharp watch. "I am willing you should feed from My little bowl," He says, "but take care not to upset and break it."

COUNSELS

Our Lord loves the glad of heart, the children who greet Him with a smile. When will you learn to hide your troubles from Him, or to tell Him gaily that you are happy to suffer for Him? The face is the mirror of the soul, and yours, like that of a contented little child, should always be calm and serene. Even when alone be cheerful, remembering always that you are in the sight of the angels.

COUNSELS

I confess that the sweetest aspirations of love often come to me in the refectory. Sometimes I am brought to a standstill by the thought that were Our Lord in my place He would certainly partake of those same dishes which are served to me....I imagine myself at Nazareth, in the house of the Holy Family. If, for instance, I am served with salad, cold fish, wine, or anything pungent in taste, I offer it to Saint Joseph. To our Blessed Lady I offer hot foods and ripe fruit, and to the Infant Jesus our feast-day fare, especially rice and preserves. But when I am served a wretched dinner I say cheerfully: "Today, my little one, it is all for you."

COUNSELS

If the greatest sinner on earth should repent at the moment of death, and draw his last breath in an act of love, neither the many graces he had abused, nor the many sins he had committed, would stand in his way. Our Lord would see nothing, count nothing but the sinner's last prayer, and without delay He would receive him into the arms of His mercy.

COUNSELS

This toy [a kaleidoscope that Thérèse played with as a child] excited my admiration, and for a long time I wondered what could produce so charming a phenomenon. One day, however, a careful examination showed that it consisted simply of tiny bits of paper and cloth scattered inside. Further scrutiny revealed three mirrors inside the tube…[an] illustration of a great truth.

As long as our actions, even the most trivial, remain within love's kaleidoscope, the Blessed Trinity, figured by the three mirrors, imparts to them a wonderful brightness and beauty. The eye-piece is Jesus Christ, and He, looking from the outside through Himself into the kaleidoscope, finds all our works perfect. But, should we leave the ineffable abode of love, He would see nothing but the worthless chaff of worthless deeds.

COUNSELS

$\mathcal{B}$eing somewhat of a child in my ways, the Holy Child—to help me in the practice of virtue—inspired me with the thought of playing with Him, and I chose the game of ninepins [a game similar to bowling]. I imagined these pins of all sizes and colors, representing the souls I wished to reach. My love for the Holy Child was the ball.

COUNSELS

$\mathcal{A}$t the moment of Communion I sometimes liken my soul to that of a little child of three or four, whose hair has been ruffled and whose clothes have been soiled at play....But Our Blessed Lady comes promptly to the rescue, takes off my soiled pinafore, and arranges my hair, adorning it with a pretty ribbon or a simple flower....Then I am quite nice, and able to seat myself at the Banquet of Angels without having to blush.

CONSOLATIONS

$\mathcal{I}$s not Jesus all-powerful? Do not creatures belong to Him who made them? Why does He condescend to say: "Pray you the Lord of the harvest that He send forth laborers"? It is because the delicacy of His love for us surpasses all understanding that He wishes us to share in all He does. The Creator of the universe awaits the prayer of a poor little soul to save a multitude of other souls, ransomed, like her, at the price of His blood.

LETTER TO SISTER GENEVIEVE

*D*ryness and drowsiness—such is the state of my soul in its interactions with Jesus! But since my Beloved wishes to sleep, I will not prevent Him. I am only too happy that He does not treat me as a stranger, but rather in a homely way. He riddles His "little ball" with pin-pricks that hurt indeed, though when they come from the hand of this loving Friend, the pain is all sweetness, so gentle is His touch.

LETTER TO MOTHER AGNES OF JESUS

*T*hérèse, the little Spouse of Jesus, loves Him for Himself; she looks on the Face of her Beloved only to catch a glimpse of the tears which delight her with their secret charm. She longs to wipe away those tears, or to gather them up like priceless diamonds with which to adorn her bridal dress.

LETTER TO MOTHER AGNES OF JESUS

We must keep all for Jesus with jealous care. It is so good to work for Him alone. How it fills the heart with joy, and lends wings to the soul! Ask of Jesus that Thérèse—his grain of sand—may save Him a multitude of souls in a short space of time, so that she may the sooner behold his adorable Face.

LETTER TO MOTHER AGNES OF JESUS

For my part, I find it quite easy to practice perfection, now that I realize it only means taking Jesus captive through His heart. Look at a little child who has just vexed its mother, either by giving way to temper or by disobedience. If it hides in a corner and is sulky, or if it cries for fear of being punished, the mother will certainly not forgive the fault. But should it run to her with its little arms outstretched, and say: "Kiss me, Mother, I will not do it again," what mother would not straightway clasp the child lovingly to her heart, and forget all it had done?

LETTER TO SISTER FRANCES TERESA

$\mathcal{L}$eaving to great and lofty minds the beautiful books which I cannot understand, still less put into practice, I rejoice in my littleness because "only little children and those who are like them shall be admitted to the Heavenly Banquet" (Matthew 19:14). Fortunately, "there are many mansions in My Father's house" (John 14:2); if there were only those seemingly incomprehensible mansions with their baffling approaches, I should certainly never enter there.

LETTER TO A MISSIONARY PRIEST

$\mathcal{J}$esus has always treated me as a spoiled child....It is true that His Cross has been with me from the cradle, but for the Cross He has given me a passionate love.

LETTER TO A MISSIONARY PRIEST

$\mathcal{I}$t is possible to remain little even in the most responsible position, and besides is it not written that at the last day "the Lord will arise and save the meek and lowly ones of the earth" (Psalms 75:10). He does not say "to judge" but "to save."

LAST WORDS

$\mathcal{I}$t is the way of spiritual childhood, the way of trust and absolute self-surrender. [Thérèse responding to Mother Agnes of Jesus when asked "What is the 'little way' that you would teach?"]

LAST WORDS

DEDICATED TO OUR LADY

Dedicated to Our Lady

Though Thérèse's central devotion was to Our Lord, the Blessed Mother occupied an important place in her spiritual life. Thérèse admired Mary's simplicity, her spirit of faith, her silence, and her steadfastness in God's love. These notions fit perfectly with Thérèse's concept of the "little way."

I entered the confessional and knelt down. When the priest opened the sliding window he saw no one, for I was so small that my head came beneath the elbow rest. He then asked me to stand up. I made my confession and received absolution in a spirit of the most lively faith. I remember the priest exhorted me to be devout to Our Lady, and how I determined to redouble my love for her who already filled so large a place in my heart.

MANUSCRIPT A

*O*n reaching home [after attending Pauline's clothing day at Carmel], I became so ill that, humanly speaking, there was no hope of recovery….I remained in a strange kind of swoon, unable to make the slightest movement, and yet hearing everything that was said around me....One Sunday during the novena to Our Lady of Victories, Marie [Thérèse's sister] knelt in tears at the foot of the bed. Then, looking towards the statue of Our Lady, she implored her assistance with all the fervor of a mother who begs the life of her child and will not be refused.

Utterly exhausted, and finding no help on earth, I too sought my heavenly Mother's aid, and entreated her with all my heart to have pity on me.

Suddenly the statue became animated and radiantly beautiful—with a divine beauty that no words of mine could ever convey. The look on Our Lady's face was unspeakably kind and sweet and compassionate, but what penetrated to the very depths of my soul was her gracious smile. Instantly all my pain vanished, my eyes filled, and big tears fell silently, tears of purest heavenly joy.

MANUSCRIPT A

*I*n the afternoon, I read the Act of Consecration to Our Lady in the name of all the first Communicants....I put my whole heart into the reading of the prayer, and sought Our Blessed Lady always to watch over me. It seemed to me that she looked down lovingly, and once more smiled on her Little Flower.

I recalled the visible smile which had cured me, and my heart was full of all I now owed her, for it was no other than she who, on that very May morning, had placed in the garden of my soul her Son Jesus—the Flower of the field and the Lily of the valleys" (Song of Songs 2:1).

MANUSCRIPT A

I received the miniature lily [from her father] as a relic, and I noticed that in trying to pluck the slender blossom, Papa had pulled it up by the roots: it seemed destined to live on, but in other and more fertile soil. He had just done the same thing for me, by permitting me to leave the sweet valley of my childhood for the mountain of Carmel. I fastened my little white flower to a picture of Our Lady of Victories, so that the Blessed Virgin smiles on it and the Infant Jesus seems to hold it in His hand. It is there still.

MANUSCRIPT A

*W*hen we reached Paris, Papa took us to see all its wonders, but for me the sole attraction was the church of Our Lady of

Victories. I can never tell you what I felt at her shrine; the graces she granted me there were like those of my first Communion day, and I was filled with happiness and peace. In this holy spot, the Blessed Virgin told me plainly it was really she who had smiled on me and cured me. With intense fervor, I entreated her to guard me always, to realize my heart's desire by sheltering me under her spotless mantle, and to remove me from every occasion of sin.

MANUSCRIPT A

*T*he trial [of waiting to hear if she was accepted into Carmel] was a sore one, but He whose Heart is ever watching taught me that He works miracles for those whose faith is as a grain of mustard seed, in the hope of thereby strengthening it; while for His Mother even, He did not work wonders until He had put her faith to the test. At the marriage feast of Cana, when Our Lady asked her Divine Son to aid the master of the house, did He not answer that His hour had not yet come? But after the trial what a reward! Water was changed into wine.

MANUSCRIPT A

*W*as not the Nativity of Mary a beautiful feast on which to become the spouse of Christ? It was the little new-born Mary who presented her Little Flower to the Little Jesus. That day everything was little except the graces I received, except my peace and joy as I gazed when night came down, upon the glorious star-lit sky. [Thérèse is referring to the day of her first profession.]

MANUSCRIPT A

*P*icturing my soul as a piece of waste ground [during her thanksgiving after Communion], I beg of Our Lady to take away my imperfections, which are as heaps of rubbish, and to raise upon it a spacious pavilion worthy of heaven, and beautify it with her own adornments. I next invite all the angels and saints to sing canticles of love, and it seems to me that Jesus is pleased to find Himself welcomed with such magnificence.

MANUSCRIPT A

*T*his is my secret, I never reprimand you [Thérèse's novices] without first invoking Our Blessed Lady, asking her to inspire me with whatever will be for your greatest good. Often I am myself astonished at what I say, but as I say it, I feel I make no mistake.

COUNSELS

O Mary, were I queen of heaven, and you were Thérèse, I would wish to be Thérèse, that I might see you Queen of Heaven. [These were the last words written by the hand of Saint Thérèse.]

COUNSELS

*S*peaking of the Blessed Mother, I must tell you of one of my simple ways. Sometimes I find myself saying to her: "Dearest Mother, it seems that I am happier than you. I have you for my Mother, and you have no Blessed Virgin to love....It is true, you are the Mother of Jesus, but you have given Him to me, and He, from the Cross, has given you to be our Mother—thus we are richer than you."

LETTER TO SISTER GENEVIEVE

*H*ow I love Our Blessed Lady! How I
would have sung her praises had I been a priest!
She is spoken of as unapproachable, whereas
she should be represented as imitable....She is
more Mother than Queen.

LAST WORDS

O sweetest Star of Heaven!
O Virgin, spotless, blest Mother!
Beneath your veil let my tired spirit rest
For this brief passing day!

FROM "MY SONG OF TODAY"

I fear no more your majesty, so far removed
above me,

For I have suffered sore with you: now hear
me, Mother mild!

Oh, let me tell you face to face, dear Mary!
How I love you;

And say to you for evermore: I am Your
little child.

FROM "WHY I LOVE YOU, MARY,"
THE LAST POEM WRITTEN BY SAINT THÉRÈSE

ACCOMPLISHED IN THE SMALL WAYS OF SELF-DENIAL

Accomplished in the Small Ways of Self-Denial

One of the major characteristics of the spirituality of Saint Thérèse of Lisieux was the practice of making small sacrifices. The young saint did not create a life of austere penance and mortifications—no hair shirts, excessive fasting, or sackcloth. In fact, though she kept the Carmelite Rule with great fidelity and attention to the letter of the Rule, she wore a white velvet dress for her entry into Carmel. (This dress was later used to make the vestments for the celebration of Mass said upon her beatification.) Saint Thérèse is truly the saint of the ordinary, proving that it may take more courage to practice virtue in the small things rather than to shine at the big things. The following stories from her life illustrate her own exacting practice of the "little way."

Sacrifice was never a matter of surprise....From the very outset my path was strewn with thorns rather than roses....Our Lord permitted that Mother Mary of Gonzaga [prioress of Carmel]—sometimes unconsciously—should treat me with much severity. She never met me without finding fault, and I remember on one occasion when I had left a cobweb in the cloister she said to me before the whole community: "It is easy to see that our cloisters are swept by a child of fifteen. It is disgraceful! Go, sweep away that cobweb; and be more careful in the future." [This undertaking was a difficult one since Thérèse was deathly afraid of spiders.]

MANUSCRIPT A

*O*ur Mistress [Sister Mary of the Angels] was truly a saint, a perfect type of the first Carmelites; she had to teach me how to work, and so I was constantly with her. Yet, kind as she was, and as much as I loved and appreciated her, my soul did not expand under her guidance. Words failed me when I spoke to her of what passed in my soul, and thus my time of spiritual direction became a torture and a real martyrdom.

MANUSCRIPT A

*A*t the close of my year of novitiate, Mother Mary of Gonzaga [prioress of Carmel] told me I must not think of profession as the Superior of Carmel had expressly forbidden it, and I must wait for eight months more. Though at first I found great difficulty in being resigned to such a sacrifice, divine light soon penetrated my soul.

MANUSCRIPT A

$\mathcal{I}$ began to have a preference for whatever was ugly and inconvenient, so much so that I rejoiced when a pretty little water jar was taken from my cell and replaced by a big one, badly chipped all over. I also made great efforts not to excuse myself, but I found this very difficult.

MANUSCRIPT A

$\mathcal{I}$t happened that a small jar which had been left by a window was found broken. Believing that I was the culprit, our Novice Mistress reproached me for leaving it about, adding that I was most untidy and must be more careful for the future. She seemed displeased, so without saying a word in self-defense, I kissed the ground and promised to be more orderly.

MANUSCRIPT A

$\mathcal{O}$ne day, during recreation, the portress came to ask for a Sister to help her in some particular task. I had the eager desire of a child to do this very thing, and as it happened, the choice fell upon me. I began immediately to fold up my needlework, slowly enough, however, to allow my neighbor to fold hers before me, for I knew it would please her to take my place. Noticing how deliberate I was, the portress said laughingly: "Ah! I thought you would not add this pearl to your crown; you were too slow." And all the community were left under the impression that I had acted according to nature.

Manuscript B

To give to everyone who asks is less pleasant than to give spontaneously and of one's own accord. Again, if a thing be asked in a courteous way, consent is easy, but if, unhappily, tactless words have been used, there is an inward rebellion unless we are perfect in charity. We discover no end of excuses for refusing, and it is only after we have made clear to the guilty Sister how rude was her behavior, that we grant *as a favor* what she requires, or render a slight service which takes, perhaps, one-half of the time we have lost in setting forth the difficulties and our own imaginary rights.

Manuscript B

To lend without hope of return may seem hard; one would rather give outright, for a thing once given is no longer ours. When a Sister comes to you and says: "I have Our Mother's leave to borrow your help for a few hours, and you may rest assured that later on I will do as much for you," we may be practically certain that the time so lent will never be repaid, and therefore feel sorely tempted to say: "I will *give* what you ask!" The remark would gratify self-love, it being more generous to give than to lend, and, in addition, it would let the Sister feel how little reliance you put in her promise.

MANUSCRIPT B

Formerly, a holy nun of our community was a constant source of annoyance to me....Unwilling to yield to my natural antipathy, I endeavored to treat this Sister as I would my most cherished friend....I did not rest satisfied with praying earnestly for the Sister who gave me such occasions for self-mastery, but I tried also to render her as many services as I could; and when tempted to make a disagreeable answer, I made haste to smile and change the subject of conversation.

MANUSCRIPT B

The noise we made awoke you [Mother Mary of Gonzaga, who was suffering from acute bronchitis], and the blame was cast upon me. I was burning to defend myself when happily it occurred to me that if I began to do so, I should certainly lose my peace of mind, and that as I had not sufficient virtue to keep silence when accused, my only chance of safety lay in flight. I fled but my heart beat so violently that I could not go far and I had to sit down on the stairs to taste the fruits of my victory. This is without doubt an odd kind of courage, yet I think it better not to expose oneself in the face of certain defeat.

MANUSCRIPT B

When I am talking with a novice I am ever on the watch to mortify myself, avoiding all questions which would tend to gratify my curiosity. Should she begin to speak on an interesting subject, and leaving it unfinished pass on to another that wearies me, I am careful not to remind her of the digression, for no good can come of self-seeking.

MANUSCRIPT B

$\mathcal{B}$efore when I saw a Sister doing something I did not like, and seemingly contrary to our rule, I used to think how glad I should be if I could only warn her and point out her mistake. But since it has become my duty to find fault [as novice mistress], my ideas have undergone a change. Now, when I see something wrong I heave a sign of relief. I thank God the guilty one is not a novice and that it is not my business to correct her; then I do all I can to find excuses, and to credit her with the good intentions she no doubt possesses.

MANUSCRIPT B

$\mathcal{I}$conclude that I ought to seek the companionship of those Sisters for whom I feel a natural aversion, and try to be their good Samaritan. It frequently needs only a word or a smile to impart fresh life to a despondent soul.

MANUSCRIPT B

$\mathcal{B}$efore Sister St. Peter became quite helpless, someone had to leave the evening meditation at ten minutes to six and take her to the refectory. Aware of the difficulty, or rather the impossibility, of pleasing the poor invalid, it cost me a great effort to offer my services....I humbly offered my help, which was accepted, though only after considerable persuasion.

MANUSCRIPT B

*F*or a long time, my place at meditation was near a Sister who fidgeted incessantly, either with her rosary or with something else. Possibly I alone heard her because of my very sensitive ear, but I cannot tell you to what an extent I was tried by the irritating noise. There was a strong temptation to turn around and with one glance silence the offender; yet in my heart I knew I ought to bear with her patiently, for the love of God first of all, and also to avoid causing her pain. I therefore remained quiet, but the effort cost me so much that sometimes I was bathed in perspiration, and my meditation consisted merely in the prayer of suffering.

MANUSCRIPT B

*O*n one occasion when I was engaged in the laundry, the Sister opposite to me, who was washing handkerchiefs, kept splashing me continually with dirty water. My first impulse was to draw back and wipe my face in order to show her that I wanted her to be more careful. The next moment, however, I saw the folly of refusing treasures thus generously offered, and I carefully refrained from betraying any annoyance. On the contrary, I made such efforts to welcome the shower of dirty water that at the end of half an hour I had taken quite a fancy to the novel kind of aspersion.

MANUSCRIPT B

When we are guilty of a fault we must never attribute it to some physical cause, such as illness or the weather. We must ascribe it to our own imperfections, without being discouraged by it. "Occasions do not make a person frail, but show what he is."

COUNSELS

God did not permit that our Mother [the prioress] should tell me to write my poems as soon as I had composed them, and I was so afraid of committing a sin against obedience that I would not ask permission for this. So I had to wait for some free time, and at eight o'clock in the evening I often found it extremely difficult to remember what I had composed in the morning.

COUNSELS

If your desire is to draw great profit, do not go to recreation with the idea of enjoying yourself, but with the intention of entertaining others and practicing self-denial. Thus, for instance, if you are telling one of the Sisters something you think entertaining, and she should interrupt to tell you something else, show yourself interested, even though in reality her story may not interest you in the least. Be careful, also, not to try to resume what you were saying. In this way you will leave recreation filled with a great interior peace and endowed with fresh strength for the practice of virtue.

COUNSELS

It is not playing the game to argue with a Sister that she is in the wrong, even when it is true, because we are not answerable for her conduct. We must not be Justices of the peace, but Angels of peace only.

COUNSELS

*W*hat gives me strength is that I offer each step [in the garden] for some missionary, thinking that somewhere far away, one of them is worn out by his apostolic labors, and to lessen his fatigue I offer mine to God." [Thérèse responding to a sister who pointed out that the ill saint had been instructed by the infirmarian not to walk in the garden.]

LAST WORDS

*D*uring my postulantship, it cost me a great deal to perform certain exterior penances customary in our convents, but I never yielded to my repugnance, for it seemed as though from the great crucifix in our garden Christ looked at me with beseeching eyes and begged these sacrifices.

LAST WORDS